Epitome Of Scan

Edward M Seymour

This volume is dedicated to a simplified view of scan design
which comprehends the most common applications and offers
a tie to the related math/science.

Table of Contents

About the author

I began my introduction to computing in high school so long ago the galaxy far away was not even devised. It was the age of Aquarius where freedom to experiment was rampant and wars were a thing that divided us from the establishment. Computing was sitting at a terminal remote connected via a telephone to a box at Syracuse University. This was a rare privilege to have such access and ability to "program" in Basic, Fortran or Apl. Programs were saved on stacks of cards, each having 8 characters for comment or number and 72 characters for code.

During the same era books like 1984 by George Orwell and Soylent Green by Harry Harrison were required reading. Concerns over Big Brother and associated government control dominated the landscape. This for me was my launch into the world of computing. Since then I have worked on computer development in IBM and subsequent places that have allowed me to work on processors that range from Unix servers to military controllers and included a period of helping develop curriculum for undergraduate study of chip design and test along with supporting the Auto Industry and compute intense applications.

This particular book came from a series of queries on the topic and thus this could serve as a brief survey of the concept of scan and current applications. By no means is it exhaustive or necessarily complete. Au Contraire, my goal is for you, the reader, to fill in some intended blanks with observations.

Acknowledgements

My philosophy of how computing could more closely match our expectations has come from decades of study. Study, in the strict sense has been an amazing split of classroom, laboratory merged with an art form called people watching. One could say it is the last element where I have gained the most. In essence it is as though I have been an apprentice in several disciplines. It has been a form of "learn from others mistakes, successes, break evens". While the list of others is literally much too long to reasonably include, I must mention with great appreciation the encouragement and perspective I have gained from a select few people.

My first thanks go to my supportive wife and family without whose support, none of this would be possible. In the realm of family a special tribute goes to my Mom, Doris Seymour. While she left us in 2004, she left behind such a legacy. She was, first and foremost, an acute observer of human behavior, where her means for recording this was poetry. For as long as she was alive she wrote 2-3 poems a day and handed them out to random people crossing here path. Upon her death, she handed me that baton. A chronicle of her amazing life will be the subject of another volume.

Next up, my Dad, Mason Seymour, taught me that compassion and love were best expressed in actions. Words for him were measured and carefully dispensed but actions speak louder than words rang so true. His capacity for love and compassion was unlimited, even in the face of adversity. He was a strong believer in Fate and the idea that each of us was on a path, predetermined.

Enter my Mom's mother, maternal grandmother, Sarah Southworth, who had survived a harsh life. For her the depression was a painful experience where she lost a daughter while the daughter was giving birth, gave her only son to tragedy in World War II, nearly lost my mom to sickness and was hopelessly addicted to caffeine. She was amazingly unflappable but held a hard line on one concept, never tell her that you can't do something. The result is, out comes the lecture.

Jack Mosher came next as imitation Grandfather. This was due to the following factors. All other biological grandparents had died before I was born. In addition, Jack had this innate curiosity and passion for life. His contribution to this collection was the value of using correct, simple tools whenever you can. His ability to pull one's gullible leg and use humor of catastrophe has stuck with me to this day.

Andre Lepine came into our lives as a French Canadian bushman who taught Agriculture at my school. From him I gained immense respect for mother nature, ability to identify plants and trees along with some of the most novel ways to employ them. To his credit I got immersed in French. To his credit, he had a devious way to coerce teenagers to gain respect for their own ability and worth. He was also a miracle worker with rough, unsawn wood.

IBM

Ed Eichelberger and Tom Williams

Inside IBM these two people were credited with creation of LSSD. At the time I was first introduced to them and the concepts, the ideas were considered IBM secrets. To run the IBM VLSI Academic Program required me to help divine a way to express these concepts in a manner digestible by an undergraduate student while not disclosing secrets. This was my first entry into creating text books and meant I had the honor of having these brilliant guys review and approve. IEEE later conferred them many honors including the ones mentioned below:

https://www.computer.org/web/awards/mcdowell-eichelberger-williams

http://www.synopsys.com/Tools/Implementation/RTLSynthesis/Pages/Power-Test-Ad.aspx

Rochester Institute of Technology

http://www.rit.edu/ was where I learned that the study of math and science form a gateway through which one could apply critical thinking skills. Firmly embedded in the DNA of the place was the insistence on practicing the craft of which you study. In this test drive of a career path, you either affirm or deny life long interests. It was a private university with vocational focus and demand of excellence.

Dr Kenneth Hsu

https://people.rit.edu/kwheec/homepage.html was a passionate junior professor when he joined our fray at RIT. In time, it became clear that what he lacked in English skills was completely compensated by his depth of knowledge in computer architecture and computer systems. As his first class of cynical students, we were unkind and unforgiving. We even developed a hash table to translate a language we phrased as Ah Chu into English.

Dr Roy Czernikowski

https://www.linkedin.com/in/roy-czernikowski-3aa0ba7a?authType=NAME_SEARCH&authToken=IDq2&local e=en_US&trk=tyah&trkInfo=clickedVertical%3Amynetwork%2 CclickedEntityId%3A280928434%2CauthType%3ANAME_SE ARCH%2Cidx%3A1-2-2%2CtarId%3A1473781947738%2Ctas%3ARoy%C2%A0Czerni kowski

He was the mad man behind a revolution called Computer Engineering. His method of validating that you listened in class was Baptism by fire followed by a walk on hot coals. His passion was real time computing and it came with a focus on what you could do with 100 lines of code or less. This included programming to avoid train collisions while maximizing the speed of trains on a collision course.

Dr Roger Heinz

Dr Heinz was a large, imposing German genius who demanded deep comprehension of electronics that was co-requisite with use of higher level math. His job as instructor seemed to be two fold. Put the wrath of gods in your mind. Then listen, observe and obtain the core idea by means of visualizing a solution via simple graphs. Know your derivations was a bonus when bored.

Dr Lynn Fuller

https://people.rit.edu/lffeee/

Dr Fuller has been a force at RIT that helped form the microelectronics program. His inspiration, and largely mine, came from a fire ball called

Dr Baker

was an inspiration to many who followed. His was the thick film microelectronic program which layed the groundwork for the semiconductor fab I got to use.

Dr Henri Banerjee

Author of the text simply know as Modern Physics invited me as a Junior to participate in some PN junction theoretical efforts to analytically derive boundary conditions that govern turn on voltage. This began with Fortran code I used to plot the discontinuities in prevailing theory. Selection for this effort gave me incredible motivation to continue my studies.

Penn State University

http://www.psu.edu/

Dr David Landis – (now at CMU instead)

https://www.cmu.edu/engineering/materials/people/faculty/bios/landis.html

Dave was a partner in a ground breaking effort to prove it possible to teach computer architecture, design and test to undergraduate students in the mid 1980s. (https://www.linkedin.com/in/edwardmseymour?trk=hp-identity-name) – [see publications] While student chip samples produced and validated were relatively small, it was unpredicted to see this play out in a single semester class.

University Of Illinois, Urbana–Champaign

http://illinois.edu/

Dr William Kubitz

https://cs.illinois.edu/directory/profile/kubitz

Dr Kubitz was another parter in the aforementioned program who had students creating silicon targeted at hardware implementation of software algorithms. Strictly speaking Dr Kubitz was in Computer Science department doing engineering stuff.

Dr Janak Patel

https://www.ece.illinois.edu/directory/profile/jhpatel

Dr Patel had students who tested out computer architecture in silicon. His efforts in the same program added yet another element of depth in the study of computers.

Dr Jacob Abraham

http://www.ece.utexas.edu/people/faculty/jacob-abraham

Dr Abraham was at University of Illinois when I had the pleasure to collaborate. His students were pushing new architecture thoughts in silicon as well.

University of Minnesota

https://twin-cities.umn.edu/

Dr Gerald Sobelman

http://mountains.ece.umn.edu/~sobelman/

Dr Sobelman came to the program a bit later than the others in that Minnesota was selected forth. He ha come from industry to become a professor and thus brought a different, more vocational aspect. His students had to run a gauntlet of qualifying runs before being selected for fabrication.

University of Tennesee

https://www.utk.edu/

Dr Donald Bouldin

https://www.eecs.utk.edu/people/faculty/dbouldin/

During my efforts to lead the university program, Dr Bouldin was a constant source of advice and counsel. His approach was more pragmatic as he had industry experience and that of consulting. He became a key player in my efforts to help define Mosis Tiny Chip with NSF

https://www.mosis.com/pages/products/mep/mep-about#instruct

National Science Foundation

https://www.nsf.gov

Dr Bernard Chern

https://www.nsf.gov/about/history/nsf0050/manufacturing/history.htm

Dr Chern was a leader of Mosis program in the 80s with whom I presented the idea which then morfed into Tiny Chip.

Preface

In life our actions are formed as a sum of our experience as people. This is fundamentally what sets us apart and makes us individuals. It also defines the guidebook for our journey. In this book I am not to suggest that this is the Rosetta stone, guide to making a computer actually think like us or create R2D2, Terminator or a Genie. On the contrary, this volume is dedicated to simple observations gathered, borrowed or collected over a lifetime of immersion in the world of Math, Science, computing and Anthropological study.

To prove validity of some notions within I will offer mathematical support. As time is not unlimited, I will leave proof to the reader in other areas where I have sown seeds of thought. I grew up on a farm, studies the effect of music and poetry on people. Find problem solving a blast and experiment creation a rush. Essential ideas herein are meant to be within the grasp of anyone with interest. Heretofore, consider this a book a guide book to explore scan design and its primary applications.

Scan, What Is It?

If we consider what is implied by scan, it is a cursory glance at something. Google and Webster have their own view https://www.google.com/search?q=scan&oq=scan&aqs=chrome..69i57.2651j0j7&sourceid=chrome&es_sm=93&ie=UTF-8#q=scan+definition

http://www.merriam-webster.com/dictionary/scan

In the world of testing electronics, scan implies a simple means by which electronics can be tested with great accuracy, simply, and to a large extent, efficiently. To this end, there are a few major settings in which scan is applied to make complex testing simple. In this book I will introduce common applications of scan and essentials of how they work. I will also cover some elements of design which warrant caution.

What new thing do you understand about scan and how can you relate it to a digital scanning device?

Serial Data Transmission With A Finite, Predictable Packet Size

The aforementioned are the big words to define access to internals of a design using scan methods.

Elements of any scan operation

- Scan Clock
- Scan Instruction
- Scan State Machine
- Scan Controls
- Scan Inputs
- Scan Outputs
- Scan Data

I will attempt to explain the function of each element and how they tend to vary. I will also offer some insight into commonly used methods to optimize so that one can scan quickly with accuracy.

To best illustrate this concept in a simple system used by most designs, I will begin with a brief overview of how Jtag applies to this. https://en.wikipedia.org/wiki/JTAG

In a Jtag system Scan Clock is TCK, a rising edge based clock used to perform most Jtag operations. The typical scan instruction tends to be a length of 8bits which offers 256 instructions to use (2^8). So, in this way you could express the burst length for a Jtag instruction as 8. Herein The Scan State Machine is called the JTAG State Machine, detailed well in the wiki link.

Quick, what is the minimum pin count for JTAG 1149.1 and why?

Boundary Scan

Initially JTAG was devised to perform testing of boundaries of chips with an especial focus on IO operations and health. (boundary scan)

The essential method has grown beyond the initial 4-4 pin interface to become an integral part of boot procedures in most processors. In some ways, the power of this technique lies in its simplicity and conformal methods of access. In essence, regardless of the design, most applications adhere to the core standard of IEEE 1149.1
https://standards.ieee.org/findstds/standard/1149.1-2013.html

or some more recent variant like 1149.6 or 1149.7. engines work on instructions and or data, Instructions tend to be of fixed length given the design. Data packets or registers tend to be of variable length, defined by the sequence, precisely whose location in a design is also asserted with an address.

What does boundary scan uniquely offer?

Design For Test

Assume you want to create a complex chip to run a cell phone or a chip to run guidance of your car. Chances are you will be intolerant of processors which are miscreant. It will also require the use of N cores and M GPUs in that they are now commoditized (available as commercially IP). Given this complexity you want to test this device to ensure correct manufacture and selectively decide if and when to repair it.

Imagine as well that you want to perform these tests in such a way that you want your circuit to evaluate its own health and essential elements. We as people undergo simple tests which help us be cognizant of out overall health. We check pulse, heart rate, respiration. These are simple checks that do not require much in the way of instruments and are largely comprehensive.

The analogy in electronics of the self check for health is called DFT (design for test). Some would characterize these elements of design as a duty or tax. To that I would respond that these elements can take a complicated task of stimulation and observation and transform it into the check for a pulse, integration over time or area under a curve. The result of this summation or sampling is a figure of merit. We want to conclude works or does not work. If it fails we ask, how badly and can it be still used.

This branch of science is based on a storage element called a latch. A latch (http://vlsi-doubts.blogspot.com/2013/09/dft-q-part-14.html#gsc.tab=0) is a device whose job in life is to sample a value in time and hold it until told to release not unlike when you press on a blood vessel to "take your pulse" For that test to have accuracy, you need to hold you finger in place with constant pressure over time and you tend to time average the response to arrive at an average value. In electronics, the analogy is sampling with a string of clock pulses.

Often, the magnitude of testing is such that some deem it impossible to check the result of this testing by reviewing it visually so schemes of self test have been devised which run an algorithm in hardware and report a pass or fail condition. This is called built in self test (BIST) https://en.wikipedia.org/wiki/Built-in_self-test Some of these test algorithms include mechanisms for repair or customized settings called repair or training. https://www.mentor.com/products/silicon-yield/multimedia/overview/memory-bist-and-repair-the-industry-leading-memory-built-in-self-test-tool-for-high-quality-embedded-test-b33b5842-7033-4952-9d54-d341b4aefda1

http://arrc.ou.edu/~rockee/RIO/serialio-book.pdf

These embedded examples are simply to give you a place to start and will vary with vendor or paper. With this as a backdrop, I will now begin to introduce some new ways to look at old tests. Most of this is the result of experience, some from simple observation and mostly because for me one should consider doing the math on a regular basis.

Why Built In Self Test?

Then and Now Latches (flops)

See this discussion of LSSD and Mux D
http://abhiramsr.blogspot.com/2011/11/lssd-vs-muxd-cell-which-is-better.html Having been within IBM for quite some time I maintained a preference for LSSD design but had to develop a tolerance for Mux D. In fact, with rare exception today, Mux D is dominant.

Pros and Cons Of Mux D Vs LSSD

Electronics Do The Math

Regardless of which you choose implement, you can view a design as having a number of Zflops which tend to be arranges in Y scan chains arranged in a variety of compression methods largely based on XOR. XOR, arranged carefully with latches, does polynomial division
https://books.google.com/books?id=r8ziBwAAQBAJ&pg=PA93&lpg=PA93&dq=polynomial+division+with+a+misr&source=bl&ots=tJykY3ASMw&sig=9RZuTgy5MDDRp7em4_SiIxKQnLg&hl=en&sa=X&ved=0ahUKEwjsz8DiqpbPAhUM0WMKHf-sCIAQ6AEIUzAH#v=onepage&q=polynomial%20division%20with%20a%20misr&f=false

Why do we care about polynomial division?

What Do You Next Want To Discuss?

How Can You Apply This?

Improvements To These Ideas?

New Ways To Use This

What Needs More Explanation

How Is This Tied To A Visual Scan

www.ingramcontent.com/pod-product-compliance
Lightning Source LLC
Chambersburg PA
CBHW021857170526
45157CB00006B/2493